Reptiles

LORI BAKER • ANDREA ROY

Editorial Board
David Booth • Joan Green • Jack Booth

Steck-Vaughn®

HOUGHTON MIFFLIN HARCOURT

10801 N. Mopac Expressway
Building # 3
Austin, TX 78759
1.800.531.5015

Steck-Vaughn is a trademark of HMH Supplemental Publishers Inc.
registered in the United States of America and/or other jurisdictions.
All inquiries should be mailed to HMH Supplemental Publishers Inc.,
P.O. Box 27010, Austin, TX 78755.

Rubicon
www.rubiconpublishing.com

Project Editors: Miriam Bardswich, Kim Koh
Editorial Assistants: Kermin Bhot, Amy Land
Art/Creative Director: Jennifer Drew
Assistant Art Director: Jen Harvey
Designers: Elizabeth Ann Cannom, Gabriela Castillo, Patrick Sitlington
Cover image–StockXchange; title page–iStockphoto.com

Printed in Singapore

ISBN: 978-1-4190-2392-7
6 7 8 9 10 11 12 13 14 15   2016   24 23 22 21 20 19 18 17 16 15
A B C D E F G

CONTENTS

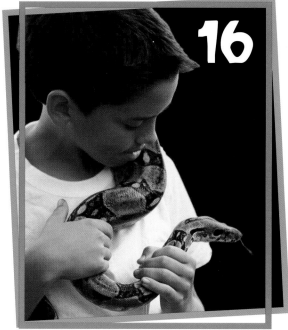

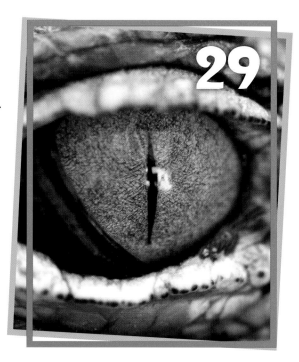

Reptiles

By Meish Goldish

Reptiles are crocodiles,
Turtles and snakes.
To be called a reptile
Here's what it takes:
Be a cold-blooded creature,
Have dry, scaly skin;
Breathe with your lungs,
Breathe out and breathe in.

Reptiles are alligators,
Tortoises, and lizards,
Hiding in the desert
From hot, sandy blizzards.
Some say that dinosaurs
Were reptiles long ago.
What is a reptile?
Well, now you know!

What Is a Reptile?

warm up

Think of reptiles that people keep as pets at home. Do you think this is a good idea? Why or why not?

A reptile is a cold-blooded animal. This means that its body becomes warm or cold depending on the temperature outside. To keep its body at the right temperature, a reptile warms up in the sun or cools down in the shade. Like birds, most reptiles hatch from eggs that are laid on land. They breathe with their lungs like human beings do.

Did you know that reptiles are related to dinosaurs? Today there are thousands of different types of reptiles on Earth.

Types of Reptiles

Turtles and Tortoises

They have a bony shell, which protects their insides. They have four legs. Turtles live mostly in water, and tortoises live on land.

Snakes and Lizards

There are 2,500 different types of snakes and 3,000 different types of lizards on Earth! They have long bodies and are covered with scales. All snakes are legless. Most lizards have four legs but some don't have any legs at all.

Crocodiles and Alligators

They are usually the largest of reptiles. They have thick horny skin, and bony plates along their backs. They have big jaws with sharp teeth and long, powerful tails.

When alligators close their mouths, their lower teeth cannot be seen. But you can see a crocodile's lower teeth even if his mouth is shut tight.

Tuatara

They look like lizards. They live on small islands near New Zealand. Tuataras have a row of spines from the head to the top of the tail. They live in burrows under the ground. They sleep all day and come out at night to eat insects and snails. The tuatara is the only living member of a group of reptiles that lived about 200 million years ago.

burrows: *holes or tunnels*

wrap up

Create a chart that lists each of the above four groups of reptiles and their features.

Discovering Dinosaurs

warm up

In a group, make a list of all the dinosaur facts you know.

Millions of years before humans existed, dinosaurs ruled the Earth for over 150 million years.

There were about 700 different types of dinosaurs. Some dinosaurs were very large. They could be as long as two large school buses and as tall as a four-story building. One of the biggest dinosaurs, the brachiosaurus (BRACK-ee-uh-SAWR-us), could be as long as 75 ft. Others like the compsognathus (komp-sog-NAY-thus) were as small as a chicken.

Some dinosaurs loved to chomp on meat. They were carnivores. They ate other dinosaurs, lizards, fish — anything with a backbone. Other dinosaurs were herbivores who ate only plants.

Dinosaurs had different types of skin:
1. Skin that was thick and bumpy.
2. Skin that had horns, spikes, and even frills.
3. Skin that acted like armor.

Some dinosaurs even had feathers.

---

armor: *protective covering*

CHECKPOINT
Why aren't dinosaurs living today?

There are a lot of different explanations for why dinosaurs became extinct. Most scientists believe it was because an asteroid hit Earth. This created major changes in the weather and the land. Dinosaurs could not survive these changes and began to die off.

---

extinct: *when all the animals of that type are dead*
asteroid: *chunk of rock revolving around the sun*

:FYI
Dinosaur is from two Greek words that mean "terrible lizard."

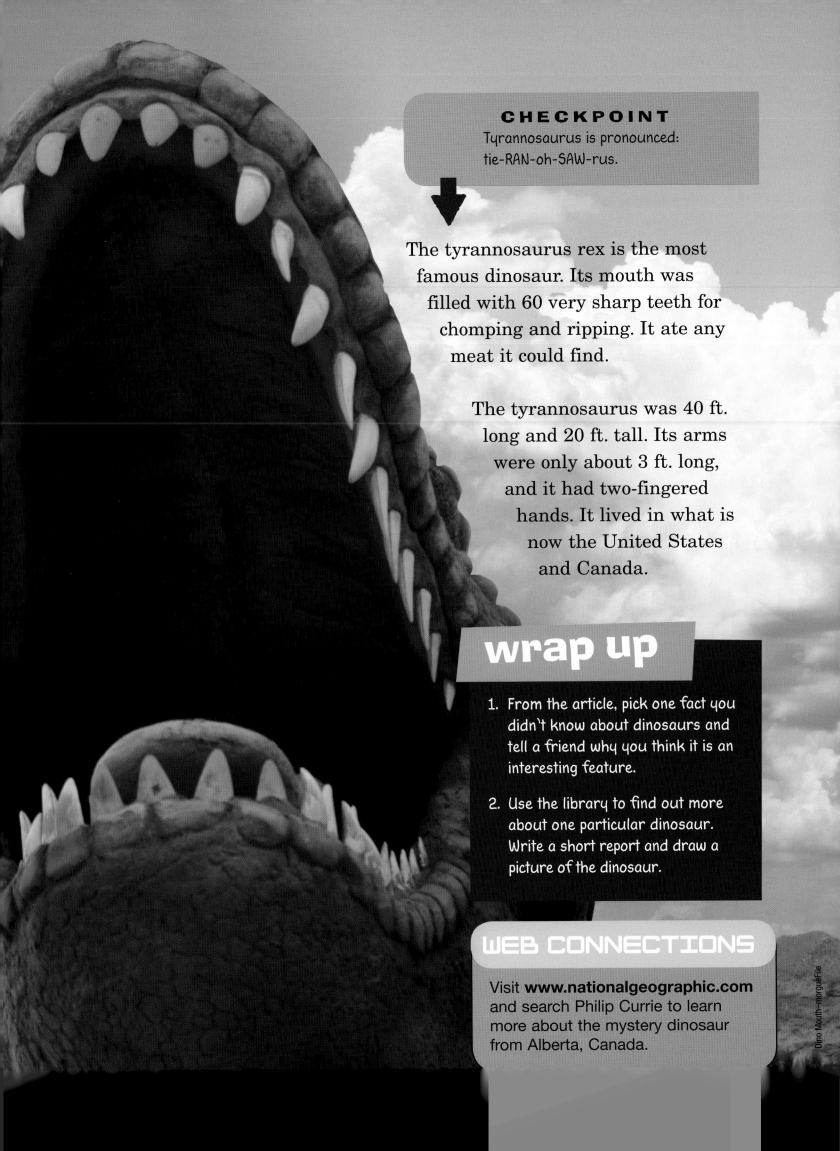

CHECKPOINT
Tyrannosaurus is pronounced:
tie-RAN-oh-SAW-rus.

The tyrannosaurus rex is the most famous dinosaur. Its mouth was filled with 60 very sharp teeth for chomping and ripping. It ate any meat it could find.

The tyrannosaurus was 40 ft. long and 20 ft. tall. Its arms were only about 3 ft. long, and it had two-fingered hands. It lived in what is now the United States and Canada.

wrap up

1. From the article, pick one fact you didn't know about dinosaurs and tell a friend why you think it is an interesting feature.

2. Use the library to find out more about one particular dinosaur. Write a short report and draw a picture of the dinosaur.

WEB CONNECTIONS

Visit **www.nationalgeographic.com** and search Philip Currie to learn more about the mystery dinosaur from Alberta, Canada.

Dino Mouth—morgueFile

Little Dragons

There are thousands of different lizards. Iguanas, chameleons, and geckos are just a few types of lizards. Lizards can be found all around the world. They do not live in very cold places. Lizards also avoid the deep oceans. Most lizards will live on the ground, while some choose to live in trees or in water.

warm up

From the title, can you guess what this article will be about?

Lizards come in a variety of bright colors. They have long bodies and long tails. The other parts are small. They have a small head, a small neck, and short legs. Lizards have moveable eyelids.

This allows lizards to "blink." This is one way to tell the difference between a legless lizard and a snake!

The largest of the lizard family is the Komodo dragon. It can grow up to 10 ft. long. The smallest is a type of gecko that measures only .6 in. Lizards can live for up to 50 years.

Lizards often use camouflage as a way of hiding from predators. Their colors help them blend into their surroundings. Others have a very unusual defense — their tails can break off! When a lizard is attacked, its tail will come off, allowing the lizard to escape. The tail will grow back but it will not look the same as the original one.

camouflage: *colors or patterns that help something hide*

When a lizard is attacked, its tail will come off!

Lizards enjoy a variety of food in their diets. They eat small mammals, birds, reptiles, frogs, eggs, and insects. Lizards use their tongues to smell food and to find enemies.

Many different types of lizards are endangered. For a variety of reasons, the number of lizards in the wild is decreasing. The destruction of their natural homes is one reason. Another reason is that lizards are sold as pets. Some people even sell them for their skins even though it is illegal.

endangered: *something that is in danger of disappearing forever*

[Frill-necked lizard–kkaplin; chameleon–Eric Isselée; desert–kavram] Shutterstock.com

: FYI

A lizard sheds its top layer of skin. This process is called "molting." By shedding the top layer of skin the lizard is able to grow.

wrap up

1. List the characteristics of lizards mentioned in this article.

2. Write a short story about a lizard that lost its tail.

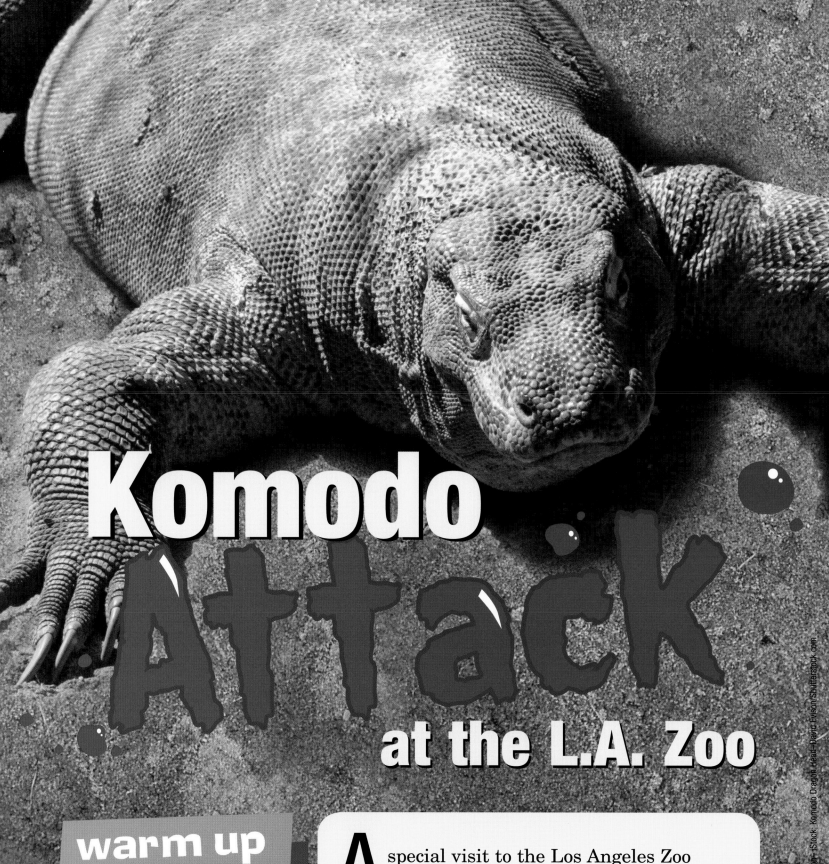

Komodo Attack
at the L.A. Zoo

warm up

Do you think Komodo dragons like to eat meat or vegetables? Make a guess!

A special visit to the Los Angeles Zoo turned into a dangerous attack for Phil Bronstein, the Executive Editor of the *San Francisco Chronicle*. He was given permission by the Los Angeles Zoo to visit the cage of the Komodo dragon. This was a gift from his then-wife, actress Sharon Stone.

The zookeeper asked Mr. Bronstein to remove his white shoes and socks because the Komodo dragon is fed white mice. Mr. Bronstein entered the cage of the Komodo dragon after removing his shoes and socks. But the Komodo dragon attacked him anyway, using its sharp teeth to bite and tear his foot!

Mr. Bronstein bravely forced open the jaws of the reptile to release his foot. He then quickly left the Komodo dragon's cage. He had to have surgery to repair the damage to his foot. He was also treated at the hospital with antibiotics to help prevent infection.

The Komodo dragon is an endangered animal. This friendly looking lizard can grow up to 10 ft. in length. With its quick speed and rows of sharp teeth the Komodo dragon is an animal to avoid!

CHECKPOINT
Why did Mr. Bronstein have to remove his white shoes and socks?

FYI

Komodo dragons have a great sense of smell. Using their tongues, they can pick up a scent one mile away. A Komodo dragon can stretch its jaw to swallow large pieces of food.

Komodo dragons will eat anything they can catch or find. Deer, goats, and even other lizards are parts of their diet. They have been known to kill people.

Did you know that the Komodo dragon can eat up to 80% of its body weight in one meal?

wrap up

1. Create a caution poster warning zoo visitors not to enter the cage of the Komodo dragon.

2. With a partner, discuss whether or not visitors should be allowed in the animals' cages. Make a list of reasons for both sides of the argument.

Slippery, Slithery Snakes

What is a snake's favorite subject in school? His-s-s-story! Do you know any other snake jokes?

There are over 2,500 different types of snakes living all over the world. You can find them in forests, deserts, and even oceans.

wrap up

1. What senses do snakes have to tell them about their environment? List them.

2. Write a paragraph about the different ways snakes can protect themselves.

Looking for Food

A snake's senses don't really work like ours do. Snakes are totally deaf (they don't have ears!) but they can sense vibrations from the ground. Snakes also don't have eyelids, just a clear scale that keeps the dirt out of their eyes. And the reason that their tongues are always flicking in and out is because they use them to pick up smells from the air.

Time for a New Skin

It may sound gross, but a snake is actually able to shed its skin. This is called molting, and it happens when the body grows and the skin becomes too tight. A molting snake will rub its head against the ground until the old skin splits open. It then slithers out of the old skin revealing shiny new scales.

Watch Out!

Most snakes are harmless, but there are a few that are very dangerous. Constrictor snakes wrap themselves around their prey until they can no longer breathe. Other snakes protect themselves with sharp fangs that inject deadly venom into their victims.

venom: *poison*

Did You Know?

warm up

Think of one fact that you already know about each of the following: lizards, crocodiles, snakes, turtles.

Lizards

Horned Lizard

• The Texas horned lizard is a fierce-looking reptile. It has scary horns and spikes all over its body. It also has another unusual form of defense. It squirts blood from its eyes to keep away predators!

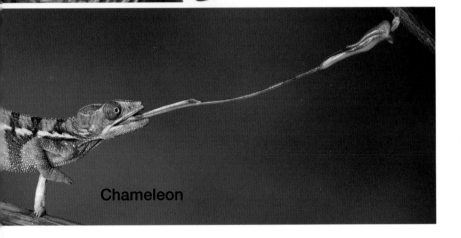

Chameleon

• The chameleon has a sticky tongue that is up to one-and-a-half times as long as its body. It uses it to capture an insect and zip it into its mouth within one-tenth of a second.

• When the yellow bearded dragon is threatened it exposes its "beard." As it flares its throat, pointed scales stand on end.

Yellow Bearded Dragon

18

Desert Tortoise

Turtles & Tortoises

• A desert tortoise can live for a whole year on what a crow eats in a single day!

• A turtle can hold its breath for several weeks or even a few months! When the weather becomes too cold for the turtle, it burrows deep into the ground. So how does it breathe when it's buried? It takes in air through its skin, throat, and an opening under its tail.

burrows: *digs*

Crocodiles & Alligators

• When they get hot, crocodiles rest with their mouths wide open. Sometimes birds will come and pick leftover food from between their teeth.

• In the wild, alligators usually run away from other animals.

• About 120 million years ago crocodiles were 40 ft. long, and they ate dinosaurs!

Nile Crocodile

Snakes

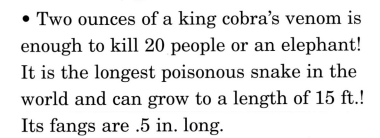

• Two ounces of a king cobra's venom is enough to kill 20 people or an elephant! It is the longest poisonous snake in the world and can grow to a length of 15 ft.! Its fangs are .5 in. long.

• How does a snake charmer charm a snake? We see the snake swaying in time to the music of the charmer's flute and believe it has been charmed. Actually, because snakes are deaf, it is just trying to keep its eyes on the charmer's swaying body!

wrap up

1. Discuss with a partner what you found surprising about snakes.

2. Choose one fact from this article and create a comic strip (graphic story) to explain this fact using pictures and text.

WEB CONNECTIONS

Fact or fiction? Use the Internet to find another interesting fact about lizards, crocodiles, snakes, or turtles. Once you have your fact, make up something that is not true about snakes. Read both to your classmates. Can they guess which one is true and which one is not true?

Snakes

By Meish Goldish

For heaven's sake, so many snakes!
Garter snakes, cobras,
Milk snakes, rat snakes,
Copperheads, pythons,
Thin snakes, fat snakes!
King snakes, bull snakes,
Water snakes, tree snakes,
Vipers and rattlesnakes,
And many-more-to-see snakes!
For heaven's sake, so many snakes!!!

A Herpetologist! What IS That?

warm up

Would you like to work with reptiles? Why or why not?

A herpetologist is a scientist who studies amphibians and reptiles. Dr. Jesus Rivas wanted to be one since he was a little boy. As a child he wished he could study the snakes that lived close to his home. His parents warned him never to touch any of the reptiles. They lived in Venezuela where many of the snakes are poisonous.

Dr. Rivas holding an anaconda.

Dr. Rivas read many books about snakes when he was young. He also kept a nature diary. In his diary he drew the reptiles he found interesting. As a teenager, he decided to volunteer at his local zoo. There he helped feed the animals and clean the cages. He always loved watching the snakes, especially the anacondas. Watching the anacondas gulp down their dinners made him want to study them even more. He decided to study biology at university.

After finishing university, Dr. Rivas became a herpetologist. He spent a lot of time studying iguanas. Then one day, his dream job came along. The Wildlife Conservation Society was looking for a herpetologist to study green anacondas.

FYI

Anacondas are the biggest snakes in the world. They can be 10-33 ft. long. They can live for 10-30 years. Anacondas are constrictors. They wrap themselves around their prey until the prey stops breathing. Then it is snack time! Anacondas mostly eat fish, birds, and turtles.

CHECKPOINT

Why are the anacondas lucky?

Luckily for the anacondas, Dr. Rivas got the job. He is able to capture an anaconda and calm it down without hurting the snake or himself.

The only tools he uses are cotton socks and very strong tape. Once the snake is quiet he measures its length. He also takes samples of the snake's blood and tissue. He gathers information about the snake so that we can learn more about them. The snake is then returned to the wild.

In the last 11 years, Dr. Rivas has captured more than 900 anacondas. The snakes he catches often weigh between 80-100 lb. Dr. Rivas uses his bare feet to find anacondas in the wild. He says he does this because he can easily feel the snakes with his bare feet. He knows what the snakes' texture and shape feel like against his skin.

Can you imagine trying to feel for a snake in murky water filled with leeches? You feel something rough and scaly slither under your toes. Was it a stick, a fish … an anaconda? You would then grab the snake with all your strength as it fights you. If these are the kinds of things that interest you, then maybe a job in herpetology is right for you!

wrap up

1. What kind of characteristics would a herpetologist need to have? Use Dr. Rivas as an example.

2. With a partner, create a list of questions you would want to ask Dr. Rivas.

The Dinner Party

Adapted from *The Dinner Party* by Mona Gardner

Who do you think would scream louder when they see a snake — boys or girls? Or, would there be no difference? Take a poll of your classmates.

SOMEWHERE IN INDIA ...

IT IS WONDERFUL TO BE IN INDIA. THANK YOU COLONEL AND MRS. WYNNES, FOR HAVING ME AS YOUR GUEST.

WE ARE SO PLEASED THAT YOU COULD JOIN US FOR DINNER.

A SPECIAL WELCOME TO MR. JONES, A NATURALIST FROM AMERICA.

THE CONVERSATION EVENTUALLY TURNS TO DEBATE:

... I TELL YOU, MOST WOMEN WILL JUMP AND SCREAM AT THE SIGHT OF A MOUSE!

I STRONGLY DISAGREE WITH YOU, SIR. WOMEN ARE STRONG, AND MOST OFTEN, CALM.

Illustrated by JEREMY BENNISON

BUT YOU ARE WRONG, MISS. A WOMAN WILL SCREAM AT ANY CRISIS!

AND A MAN?

A MAN MAY WISH TO SCREAM, BUT HE CAN CONTROL HIMSELF. THAT IS THE DIFFERENCE!

MR. JONES NOTICES SOMETHING IS WRONG WITH MRS. WYNNES ...

SHE WHISPERS SOMETHING TO THE SERVANT.

I WONDER WHAT'S WRONG WITH MRS. WYNNES? WHY DOES SHE LOOK SO TENSE?

A BOWL OF MILK! THAT CAN MEAN ONLY ONE THING. ... THERE IS A SNAKE LOOSE IN THE ROOM. A BOWL OF MILK IS BAIT FOR A COBRA ...

I DON'T SEE THE COBRA IN THE RAFTERS OR THE CORNERS OF THE ROOM. WHERE COULD IT BE?

MR. JONES REALIZES ... *IT MUST BE UNDER THE TABLE!!!*

EXCUSE ME!

I'M CURIOUS TO KNOW JUST WHAT KIND OF CONTROL EVERYONE AT THIS TABLE REALLY HAS.

I WILL COUNT TO 200 AND NO ONE IS TO MOVE A MUSCLE. THOSE WHO MOVE WILL OWE ME 50 RUPEES. READY?

1, 2, 3 ...

75, 76, 77 ...

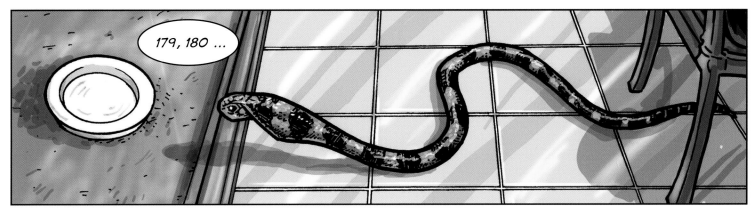

179, 180 ...

wrap up

1. Choose three adjectives to describe each of the following: Colonel Wynnes, Mrs. Wynnes, and Mr. Jones.

2. What did the colonel and the young woman argue about at the dinner party? Who do you agree with? Why? Does your class poll from the Warm Up activity support your answer?

Croc Parts

warm up

From this picture and others that you have seen, how would you describe a crocodile?

Crocodiles are found in tropical areas, usually where water meets land. The water's edge is their favorite place. Crocodiles often stay completely still with only their eyes, ears, and nose above water. They lie there watching, waiting for that thirsty wild beast to come along for a drink when suddenly: SNAP! The crocodile will grab its prey. The riverbank or shore is the perfect place for the crocodile to wait for dinner.

Crocodiles have many features that help them survive in the wild and catch their prey.

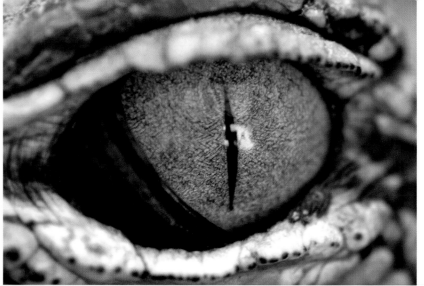

Eyes

Crocodiles have three eyelids. They have two leathery protective ones, and one clear one. Crocodiles have good eyesight even at night. They can even see under water but not very well.

Ears

They can hear very well. When crocodiles go swimming, they have a flap that covers their ears so water does not get in.

Nose

The crocodile has a good sense of smell. Its nostrils are at the top of its snout. This allows it to stay in the water while keeping just its nose above the surface.

Teeth

Crocodiles have 60–70 teeth. They do not use their teeth to chew but to clamp down on their prey. What happens if crocodiles lose their teeth? They always grow new ones so they never have to worry about being toothless.

Skin

Their skin has scales with bony sections. The bony part of the skin is like armor. It helps protect the body from attack. Crocodiles are usually black, green, or brown with black or yellow spots. A crocodile is able to hide itself in the swamp, since its skin is the same color.

Tail

A crocodile's tail is very strong. It acts like a paddle helping the crocodile swim. The crocodile makes an S-shape when it swims.

Feet

You will find two pairs of feet on a crocodile. The front pair has claws and the back pair is webbed. The feet allow the crocodile to swim, belly crawl, and walk.

CHECKPOINT
How do a crocodile's claws and webbed feet help it to move?

webbed: *toes are joined by a thin layer of skin*

wrap up

1. What characteristics allow crocodiles to survive in the wild and to capture their prey? Share your answers with a partner.

2. Imagine you could read the thoughts of the crocodile on page 29. Write down what it could be thinking.

WEB CONNECTIONS

Some people eat crocodile meat. Others use crocodile skins. Use the Internet to find out which parts are used for food and clothing.

ALLIGATOR

warm up

Have you ever heard of a dangerous animal being loose in a city? Share what happened with a partner.

:FYI

This fictional story is based on the true story of Chuckie who escaped from the Gulf Coast Zoo in Alabama, U.S. This happened when Hurricane Ivan hit the area in September 2004.

"**M**ost of the animals were sent away from the zoo before the hurricane hit. The lions, tigers, and bears were placed at other zoos." The radio announcer continued, "The zookeeper said they did not have enough time to move the alligators or the deer. Their cages were left open so they could swim away."

CHECKPOINT
Do you think it was a good idea to leave the animals' cages open?

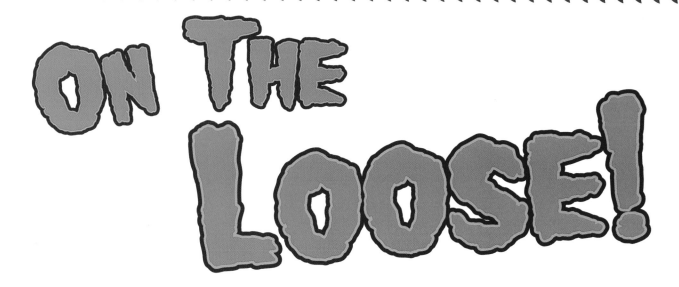

ON THE LOOSE!

My dad turned up the volume. "Chuckie, a 12-foot-long alligator weighing 900 lb., is missing. If anyone sees him, please call the police immediately."

Dad turned off the radio. "Susan, can you believe it?" he said in a loud voice. "Many people have lost their homes. There is no power. We are running out of food and now there is AN ALLIGATOR ON THE LOOSE!"

"They will find the alligator," said Mom in a calm voice.

"Who will find him? The police are too busy with other emergencies," Dad said as he rubbed his chin. He always rubbed his chin when he was worried.

There was a knock at our door.

Luke my best friend walked in.

I was so glad to see him. Everyone had been so busy cleaning up the damage from the storm that no one had time for any fun.

"Hi Luke, how is the cleanup coming?" asked Mom.

"It's coming. We're lucky that only part of the roof blew off," said Luke.

"Hey Luke, did you hear an alligator is on the loose?" I asked.

CAUTION
ALLIGATOR
ON THE LOOSE!

"Alligators can go for a year without food."

"Yeah, they said that he probably wouldn't attack. Alligators can go for a year without food. He shouldn't be hungry because he was so well fed at the zoo."

"That's the problem, Luke. He is going to be looking for his daily snack!" said Dad.

"I guess that is true," agreed Luke. "Nick, do you want to come over and play cards for a while?"

Mom looked worried. "After a storm you are supposed to stay in your house. The flood waters can be very dangerous," she said.

"Mom, it is only across the street," I said.

"Oh Susan, let the boy go," said Dad. "It's going to be like this for at least a week. He can't stay in the house the whole time."

"Great!" I said as I shoved my feet into my boots.

"Make sure that Chuckie doesn't grab you, drag you down, and swallow you boys," joked Dad as I slammed the door shut.

It felt good to get out of the house. Hurricane Ivan had hit two days ago. It sounded like a train had ripped right through our house. We had boarded the windows and bought extra food.

CHECKPOINT
Notice how the family prepared for the hurricane.

But nothing had prepared us for the damage the storm did to our town. Most of the trees had been uprooted. Many of the roofs and windows had blown away. Some houses were completely gone.

"Hey! Look at that fridge floating over there! I wonder whose it is?"

"What? Don't move! I'll go get my dad." Luke turned and ran toward his house.

"Don't leave me!" I shouted, but he was already gone. I stood frozen. Should I move? Should I run? Please let it float down the street. Please!

My heart was pounding. This can't be happening to me. I should have stayed at home. Suddenly it grabbed my leg. It was strong. It was trying to pull me down the street. I leaned the other way with all my strength. "Please, please," I thought, "just float away."

said Luke as he shook his head. All of the sudden, I felt something sharp brush against my leg. I stopped in my tracks. It started to wiggle getting closer and closer. It felt slimy and warm. Could it be Chuckie?

"Luke! I think Chuckie just grabbed me!" I yelled.

CHECKPOINT
How do you think you might act if this happened to you?

"Nick, are you okay?" shouted Luke's dad as he came running toward me. He was carrying a shovel. "Don't worry! I'll get the gator!" he said as he hit whatever was holding me.

He then yanked hard — and pulled out … a big tree branch!

"Big gator!" shouted Luke as he roared in laughter. "Let's go in and get you cleaned up."

When we got to Luke's house his mom gave us the good news. "They found Chuckie. He was swimming in a lagoon by the zoo," she said.

"Did they catch him?" I asked.

"Yes. Can you believe it took nine people to lift him into the truck? We will all sleep a little better tonight knowing that Chuckie is back at the zoo," said his mom.

I nodded my head. No one was more thankful than me.

wrap up

1. Imagine that you are Luke. Write a journal entry about Nick's experience with the "alligator." Be sure to use details from the story to make it accurate.

2. Draw a picture to go with your journal entry.

Turtle Time

warm up

Why do you think turtles have shells?

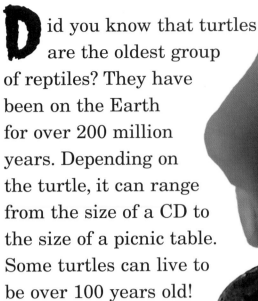

Did you know that turtles are the oldest group of reptiles? They have been on the Earth for over 200 million years. Depending on the turtle, it can range from the size of a CD to the size of a picnic table. Some turtles can live to be over 100 years old!

Painted Turtle

Check out the different types of turtles...

Craziest Names

Meet the stinkpot turtle, the river cooter, and the chicken turtle.

Endangered Turtles

It is a scary fact that 200 of the 300 different kinds of turtles are threatened with extinction. Some of the reasons include destruction of their environment, the pet trade, getting caught in fishing nets, and being used in food and medicine.

Sea Turtle

Leatherback Turtle

Best Digger

Just like the animal it's named after, the gopher tortoise loves to dig and can dig tunnels that are more than 40 ft. long!

Biggest Turtle

The leatherback turtle can reach lengths of 7.5 ft. and can weigh up to 1,100 lb. The largest leatherback found weighed 2,000 lb.

Dangerous Turtle

Snapping turtles have powerful jaws and are very fierce. They also make hissing sounds to scare off predators.

Stinkiest Turtle

The loggerhead musk turtle gives off a gross smell if it is disturbed.

Snapping Turtle in attack position

Loggerhead Musk Turtle

wrap up

1. Would you like to own any of these turtles as a pet? Why or why not? Share your reasons with the class.

2. List some of the reasons why so many turtles are in danger of becoming extinct. Design a poster that will make people aware of this problem.

WEB CONNECTIONS

Visit **www.gma.org/turtles** to learn more about turtles. Share an interesting new fact with the class.

CHEW ON THIS!

warm up

What types of things do you think reptiles eat? Compare your thoughts with a partner.

A Guide to a Reptile Lunch

We all know that reptiles enjoy a good meal. Some wait for their meals to come to them. Others will hunt for a tasty snack. Most reptiles are carnivores and will eat meat. Some prefer it alive, while others will choose whatever meat they find. Whatever reptiles choose to eat, they have one thing in common. Their bodies are especially designed for eating.

Lizards

Lizards such as the chameleon have very long tongues. This allows them to catch their meals quickly. In fact, chameleons' tongues are as long as their bodies! The iguana is mostly a herbivore. Other lizards enjoy eating mammals, insects, birds, and even other reptiles. The lizard's speed helps it catch prey quickly and easily.

herbivore: *an animal that eats plants*

Chameleon—Getty Images ; Turtle eating—stockXchange

40

Turtles

Turtles will mainly eat plants but not always. They sometimes also eat meat. The sea turtle, for example, swims to catch jellyfish, fish, and crabs. This means turtles are omnivores because they eat both plants and meat. Since turtles move slowly it is more difficult for them to catch moving prey on land.

A snake's throat makes up one-third of its body length. If a snake eats a very large meal, it can take up to one year to digest it. Snakes' jaws have special hinges so they can open their mouths very wide.

Snakes

Snakes catch and eat their prey in a variety of ways. Some are venomous. They bite their prey, releasing poison. This stops their prey from escaping so they can then swallow them. The snakes' teeth are not for chewing. They are for grabbing the prey and pulling it into the gullet. Other snakes like the boa constrictor and the python squeeze their prey before eating it. Many snakes will eat small mammals.

Snakes like the African egg-eater have a diet made up of eggs only. These snakes will eat soft-shelled eggs, like lizard eggs. Or they will eat hard-shelled eggs, like bird eggs. Soft-shelled eggs are easy to digest while hard-shelled eggs are another story! When a snake swallows a hard-shelled egg its tooth-like spine cracks the shell. The snake will then swallow the contents of the egg and spit out the shell.

gullet: *throat*

Crocodiles

Crocodiles are nocturnal hunters. This means they hunt at night. As its prey comes close, a crocodile will use its large mouth to snap it up. Crocodiles are not picky eaters. They will eat a variety of things including birds and fish.

Alligators also have a varied diet. Insects, crabs, snakes, turtles, and deer are only some of the items on their menu. Alligators will eat their food whole if it is small enough. Or they will use their strong jaws to make smaller pieces.

FYI

A crocodile's stomach is the size of a watermelon.

A crocodile usually eats about 50 times a year, which is about once a week.

Like all animals, reptiles have developed special ways of catching and eating their prey. Whether it is a snake, alligator, crocodile, lizard, or turtle, reptiles are always ready for lunch!

wrap up

1. Decide what is the best way for reptiles to catch their prey. Explain why.

2. Compare the way snakes and alligators eat their prey. Make a list of the differences and similarities.

Race

to the Finish

Snow had just begun to fall, and the winds were getting colder. The pond had also started to form a thin layer of ice. Bear was not yet ready to hibernate. So he decided to walk by the pond and see if he could find some fish. When he got there he saw something sticking out of the ice.

hibernate: *spend the winter asleep*

warm up

Have you ever been in a race? How did you feel before and after the race? Share your feelings with a friend.

"Hey there, what are you doing?"

The creature stretched its neck up and turned to look at Bear. "Why, I am preparing for winter," said a large turtle.

"Well you had better hurry!" said Bear. "Turtles move so slowly that spring will come before you are ready."

"Do you think I move slowly?" Turtle asked.

"Of course I do," Bear replied. Turtle thought for a minute and had a very interesting idea.

"Bear, would you like to have a race?"

"A race?" said Bear, and began laughing so hard that his fur shook. "You're on!" he cried.

CHECKPOINT

Why do you think Bear started laughing?

"Here is what we'll do," Turtle said. "We'll race here tomorrow morning. I will swim in the water, and you will run along the shore. The first one to reach the end wins."

Bear looked at Turtle and smiled. "Turtle, how will you swim when the pond has a thin layer of ice covering it?" Turtle returned the smile and said he would put holes in the ice so that he could pop up and take a breath. This seemed to satisfy Bear. The race was on!

On the way to his den Bear met many forest animals. He told them about the race, and they spread the word.

The next morning many animals came to watch the race. They were sure Bear would win. How could he not?

Crow started the race. "READY, SET … GO!" Bear quickly took off along the bank. His large paws bounded along the shore. As he approached the first hole he saw Turtle pop up and quickly dive down. The other animals gasped. "Did you see that? Turtle is just ahead of Bear!"

Bear dug his feet deeper into the ground and ran harder. He was panting heavily but Turtle continued to say ahead!

Exhausted, Bear collapsed at the finish line. There he saw Turtle waiting for him. The other animals stared in disbelief. They never thought Turtle would win.

Feeling miserable, Bear slowly stood up and walked back to his den. He was ready to begin his hibernation. Turtle watched the other animals leave. He then tapped on the surface of the ice. One by one a turtle appeared from each of the holes in the ice. Turtle nodded at each of the turtles. "Thank you!" he whispered.

The animals of the forest still talk about the day that Turtle beat Bear in a race.

FYI

Legends are stories that have been passed down through generations. Legends are told aloud, not written in a book.

A grizzly bear can weigh 250 to 1,100 lb.

A grizzly bear's footprint is about 6 in. wide.

wrap up

1. What lesson did Turtle wish to teach Bear and the other animals? Do you think he succeeded?

2. Think of three words to describe both Bear and Turtle's behavior during the race.

ACKNOWLEDGMENTS

The publisher gratefully acknowledges the following for permission to reprint copyrighted material in this book.

Every reasonable effort has been made to trace the owners of copyrighted material and to make due acknowledgment. Any errors or omissions drawn to our attention will be gladly rectified in future editions.

"Reptiles" from ANIMAL POEMS FROM A-Z: MORE THAN 100 RHYMES WITH RELATED ACTIVITIES by Meish Goldish. Copyright © 1994 by Meish Goldish. Published by Scholastic Inc. Reprinted by permission.

"Snakes" from ANIMAL POEMS FROM A-Z: MORE THAN 100 RHYMES WITH RELATED ACTIVITIES by Meish Goldish. Copyright © 1994 by Meish Goldish. Published by Scholastic Inc. Reprinted by permission.